SPORTING YEAR

1968

INDEX

This book gives a fascinating insight to the sports world in 1968, including football, cricket, golf, boxing, tennis, horse racing, rugby and Formula one, plus it was the year of the summer and winter Olympic.

Facts and figures about the main events in the year.

In this year:

It was the beginning of the open era in tennis when professionals could compete with amateurs in grand slam events, Wimbledon was won by Rod Laver and Billie Jean King

Manchester United won the European Cup at Wembley

In Golf, the British Open won by Gary Player

Formula One season, Graham Hill won the driver's championship driving a Lotus 49 for the second time and the last time of his career.

Sir Ivor won the 2000 Guineas and the Epsom Derby.

The 1968 Challenge Cup was won by Leeds.

There was a first Grand Slam victory for France in the 1968 Five Nations Championship.

Australia retained the Ashes after the series was drawn 1-1.

For the first time since 1937, Manchester City won the First Division Championship in football.

Jimmy Ellis won the vacant WBA Heavyweight Championship.

Sporting Names of 1968

England's football manager and captain in 1968

Sir Alfred Ernest Ramsey (22 January 1920 – 28 April 1999)

Was the England manager in 1968, when he managed England to third place in the 1968 European Championship. He was manager of England from 1963 to 1974, he guided England to victory in the 1966 World Cup, he was knighted in 1967 in recognition of England's World Cup win. As a player, Ramsey was a defender for Southampton and Tottenham Hotspur and was a member of England's 1950 World Cup squad.
As a player, Ramsey was a defender and a member of England's 1950 World Cup squad.

Robert Frederick Chelsea Moore OBE (12 April 1941 – 24 February 1993)

He was an English professional footballer. He captained West Ham United for more than ten years and was captain of the England team that won the 1966 World Cup. He is widely regarded as one of the greatest defenders of all time, and was cited by Pelé as the greatest defender that he had ever played against. He was captain of England team playing in euro's

England Cricket Captain 1968

Michael Colin Cowdrey, CBE (24 Dec 1932 – 4 Dec 2000).

Better known as Colin Cowdrey, played for Kent and England, he was the first cricketer to play 100 Test matches, celebrating the occasion with 104 against Australia in 1968. In all he played 114 Tests, making 7,624 runs at an average of 44.06. He is the fourth sportsman to be honored with a memorial service in Westminster Abbey, following Sir Frank Worrell, Lord Constantine and Bobby Moore.

He was the England captain the tour to West Indians and visit of Australia in 1968.

Winner of Formula One title in 1968.

Norman Graham Hill OBE (15 February 1929 – 29 November 1975) Graham Hill's iron-willed determination, fierce pride and great courage enabled him to overcome the odds against more naturally gifted drivers. None of them was more popular with the public than the mustachioed extrovert with the quick wit, who loved the limelight, was a natural entertainer and became one of the first Formula One media stars. He secures his second driving Formula One title in 1968.

Other Sporting names of 1968

Basil D'Oliveira, Cricketer

Rod Laver, Tennis player

Howard Winstone, Boxer

Brian Close, Cricketer

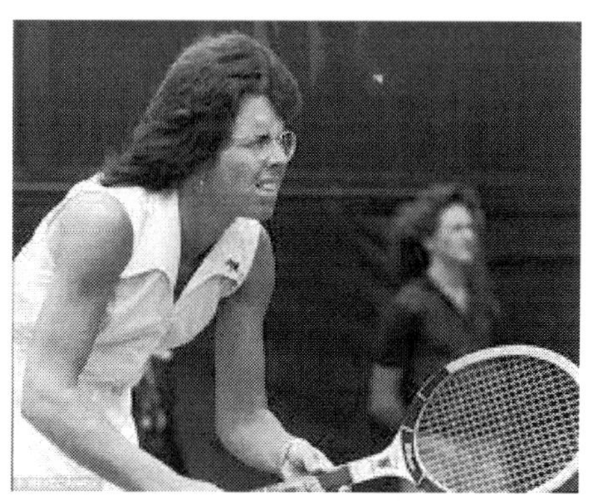

Billie Jean King, Tennis player

Billy Bremner, football

Jackie Stewart, Racing driver

Bob Beamon long jumper

Roger Hunt, Footballer

Sportsman Born in 1968

Paul Merson, born 20 March 1968, is an English former professional footballer and manager, turned football television pundit.

Mike Atherton (23 March 1968), A right-handed opening batsman for Lancashire and England, and occasional leg-break bowler. Following retirement, he became a journalist and is currently a cricket commentator with Sky Sports, and cricket correspondent of The Times.

Nasser Hussain OBE, (28 March 1968) in Madas, India, is a former English cricketer who captained the England cricket team between 1999 and 2003, with his overall international career extending from 1990 to 2004. He retired in 2004, he joined Sky Sports as a commentator shortly thereafter.

Colin Steele McRae, MBE, born 5th August 1968, was a British rally driver from Scotland. Colin McRae was the 1991 and 1992 British Rally Champion and, in 1995 won the World Rally Championship Drivers' title. McRae died in 2007 when he crashed his helicopter near his home.

Julian Andrew Dicks, born 8 August 1968, is an English former professional footballer, coach and manager.

Slaven Bilić born 11 September 1968 is a retired Croatian professional footballer and former manager of Premier League club West Ham United. Bilić had successful spells with West Ham United and Everton in England. At the international level, Bilić served as one of Croatia's most consistent defenders. He went on to manage the national side.

Didier Deschamps, born 15 October 1968 is a retired French footballer and current manager of the France national team. He played as a defensive midfielder for Marseille, Juventus, Chelsea and Valencia, as well as Nantes and Bordeaux. As a French international, he was capped on 103 occasions, captaining his nation to victories in the 1998 World Cup and Euro 2000.

Slaviša Jokanović born 16 August 1968) is a Serbian former professional footballer who played from the late 1980s to early 2000s, and is the current manager of English club Fulham. A defensive midfielder, played in Italy and England. He represented FR Yugoslavia at the 1998 World Cup and Euro 2000

Winners of 1968

Golf

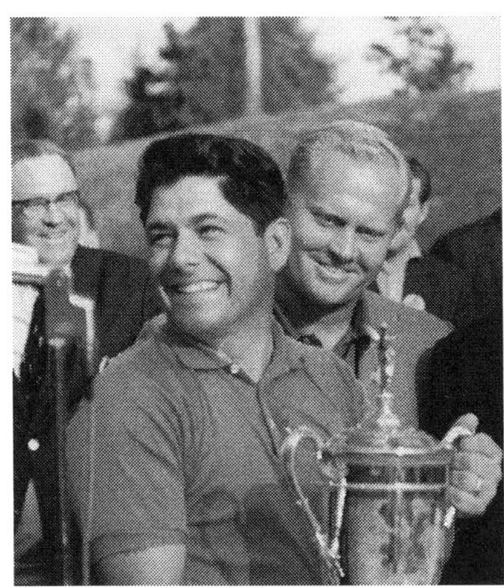

Lee Trevino
Winner of the U.S Open

Trevino won six major championships and 29 PGA Tour events over the course of his career. He twice won the U.S. Open, The Open Championship and the PGA Championship.

Julius Boros
Winner of PGA Championship

Boros won 18 PGA Tour events, including three major championships: the 1952 and 1963 U.S. Opens and the 1968 PGA Championship

Gary Player British Open Champion,

Over his career, Player accumulated nine major championships on the regular tour and six Champions Tour major championship victories

Bob Goalby Masters champion

This was his lone major championship among 11 Tour wins

Tennis

The "open era" began in 1968 when the Grand Slam tournaments agreed to allow professional players to compete with amateurs. Before 1968, only amateurs could compete in the Grand Slam tournaments and other events.

Commercial pressures and rumors of some amateurs taking money under the table led to the abandonment of this distinction, inaugurating the open era, in which all players could compete in all tournaments, and top players were able to make their living from tennis

Wimbledon Winners
Billie Jean King and Rod Laver

US Open winners
Arthur Ashe and Virginia Wade

French Open winners
Ken Rosewall and Nancy Richey

Australian Championship winners
William Bowrey and Billie Jean King

Horse Racing

Forward Pass winner of the Kentucky Derby, jockey Ismael Valenzuela

Sir Ivor won the 2000 Guineas and the Epsom Derby, jockey Lester Piggott

Ribero, winner of the St Leger, jockey Lester Piggott

Red Alligator, winner of the grand national, jockey Brian Fletcher

Vaguely Noble winner of the Prix de l'Arc de Triomphe at Longchamp, jockey Bill Williamson

Rugby League

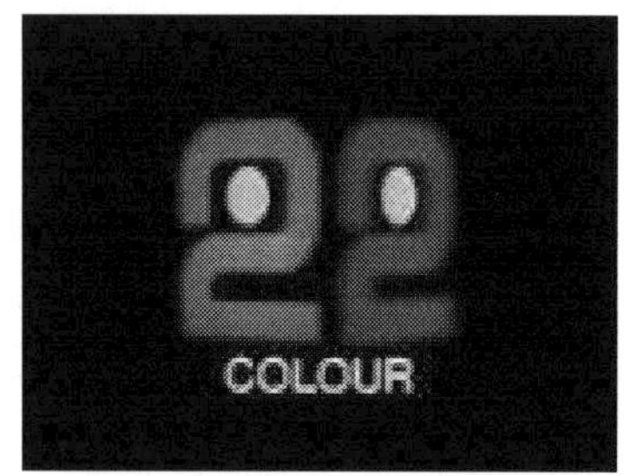

The BBC2 Floodlit Trophy winners were Castleford who beat Leigh 8-5 in the final

The 1968 Challenge Cup was the 67th staging of rugby league's oldest knockout competition, the Challenge Cup. The final was contested by Leeds and Wakefield Trinity at Wembley.

The final is best remembered for Wakefield's Don Fox missing a conversion from in front of the posts in the last minute of the game, handing Leeds an 11–10 victory

Leeds had ended the regular season as league leaders for the second successive season in the championship.

Wakefield Trinity won their second Championship, the second in successive seasons, when they beat Hull Kingston Rovers 17-10 in the Championship Final

Rugby League World Cup tournament

The 1968 Rugby League World Cup tournament was the fourth staging of the Rugby League World Cup and was held in Australia and New Zealand during May and June in 1968.

Contested by the men's national rugby league football teams of the two host countries plus Great Britain and France. The 1968 World Cup was the first to be played under limited tackles rules, the number then being four tackles. Australia and France, having finished in first and second places respectively, qualified for the World Cup final. Australia beat France 20 – 2 in the final.

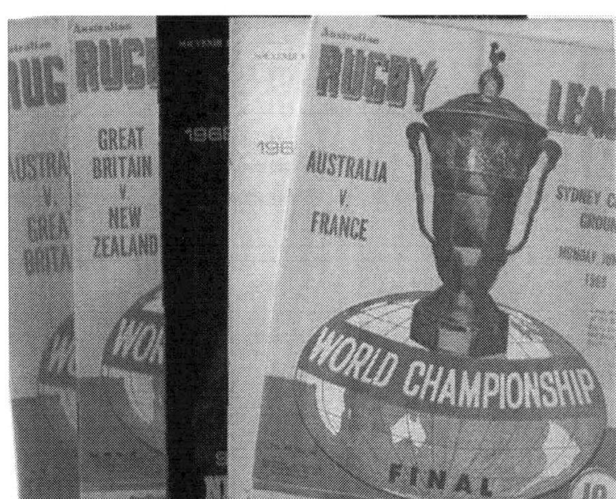

Rugby Union

The 1968 Five Nations Championship was the thirty-ninth series of the rugby union Five Nations Championship. Including the previous incarnations as the Home Nations and Five Nations, this was the seventy-fourth series of the northern hemisphere rugby union championship.

France vs Ireland

Scotland vs England

Five nations

Ten matches were played between 13 January and 23 March. It was contested by England, France, Ireland, Scotland and Wales. It marked the first Grand Slam victory for France.

Ireland vs Wales

JPR Williams, Wales

Cricket

The 1968 English cricket season was something of a watershed for it was the last in which the County Championship predominated. From 1969, a new limited overs league began, and the number of Championship matches was therefore reduced. A system of batting and bowling bonus points was introduced into the County Championship, replacing the long established 'first innings' points.

The season was also significant in being the first in which counties could sign one overseas player who would not be subject to the normal residential qualification rules but could appear for them immediately.

Most counties, with the notable exception of Yorkshire, took advantage of this. Nottinghamshire pulled off the coup of signing Garry Sobers. Other players signed were

Lee Irvine, Essex
Majid Khan, Glamorgan,
Mike Procter, Gloucestershire
Barry Richards, Hampshire
Asif Iqbal, Kent
Farokh Engineer, Lancashire
Hylton Ackerman, Northamptonshire
Greg Chappell, Somerset
Rohan Kanhai, Warwickshire
Vanburn Holder, Worcestershire

County Championship winners- Yorkshire, please note Geoff Boycott top right

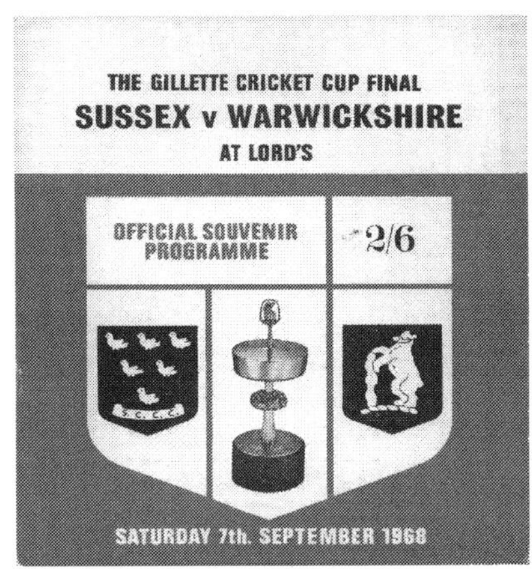

Gillette Cup winners- Warwickshire

Leading batsmen in the County Championship - Geoff Boycott topped the averages with 1487 runs @ 64.65.

The Australian cricket team toured England in the 1968 season to play a five-match Test series against England for The Ashes.
Australia retained the Ashes after the series was drawn 1-1.

Leading bowlers in the County Championship - Ossie Wheatley topped the averages with 82 wickets @ 12.95.

The England national cricket team toured the West Indies from January to March 1968 and played a five-match Test series which England won 1–0.

Football

FA Cup Final - The 1968 FA Cup Final was won by West Bromwich Albion who beat Everton 1–0 in extra time with a goal from Jeff Astle. It was Albion's fifth FA Cup success.

First Division - For the first time since 1937, Manchester City won the First Division, finishing two points clear of their local rivals Manchester United. Fulham finished in last place and were relegated along with Sheffield United. Manchester City and Manchester United qualified for European Cup, City as champions, United as the European trophy holders. Leeds United qualified for Inter-Cities Fairs Cup as the trophy holders.
Chelsea qualified for Inter-Cities Fairs Cup ahead of Everton, who finished below Liverpool, due to rule "only one club per city".

League Cup - Leeds United beat Arsenal 1–0 in the final of the League Cup to win the competition.

Newcastle United qualified for Inter-Cities Fairs Cup ahead Tottenham Hotspur and Arsenal, who finished below Chelsea, due to rule "only one club per city".

Manchester United's George Best and Ron Davies of Southampton finished as Division One's joint-top scorers with 28 goals apiece. Best was awarded the Football Writers' Association Footballer of the Year, as well as the European Footballer of the Year award.

Second Division - Bill McGarry's Ipswich Town team won the Second Division by one point from Queens Park Rangers, with both teams promoted. Blackpool finished third on goal average and so missed out. Rotherham United and bottom club Plymouth Argyle were both relegated to the Third Division.

Third Division - Oxford United won their first divisional title and achieved what was then their highest ever finish in only their sixth season as a league club. Runners-up Bury joined them in promotion. Grimsby Town, Colchester United and Scunthorpe United were relegated, although the biggest story concerned bottom placed Peterborough United who were docked 19 points for offering irregular bonuses to their players and so finished bottom. Because of the ruling Mansfield Town escaped relegation.

Fourth Division - Luton Town won the league and were promoted along with Barnsley, Hartlepool United and Crewe Alexandra. The bottom four clubs were forced to apply to re-election to the Football League as per usual; however, Port Vale were also made to apply for re-election, as a result of financial irregularities. In the end, all five clubs were re-elected.

The 1967–68 Scottish Division One was won by Celtic by two points over city rivals Rangers. Motherwell and Stirling Albion finished 17th and 18th respectively and were relegated to the 1968-69 Second Division.

Boxing

Lionel Edmund Rose MBE (21 June 1948 - 8 May 2011) was an Australian bantamweight boxer, the first Indigenous Australian to win a world title, beating Fighting Harada for the world bantamweight title on 26 February 1968 in Tokyo. On 2 July of that year, he returned to Tokyo to retain his title with a 15-round decision win over Takao Sakurai. Then, on 6 December, he met Chucho Castillo at the Inglewood Forum in Inglewood, California.

Jimmy Ellis (February 24, 1940 - May 6, 2014) faced Jerry Quarry, on April 27, 1968 in Oakland, California capture the vacant WBA Heavyweight Championship.
In his only successful title defense, Ellis defeated Floyd Patterson by a controversial 15-round decision on September 14, 1968 in Stockholm, Sweden.

Robert Lloyd "Bob" Foster (December 15, 1938 - November 21, 2015) got his first shot at a world title. At Madison Square Garden in New York, on the night of March 24, Foster became world champion by knocking out Dick Tiger in four rounds. Tiger had been a two-time world middleweight champion and was defending his world light heavyweight crown that night. Foster then decided to box at heavyweight once again, and beat future George Foreman victim Charlie Polite by a knockout in three. He ended that year defeating Vick again, and his future world title challenger Roger Rouse, both by a knockout.

Motor Racing

The 1968 Formula One season was the 22nd season of the FIA's Formula One motor racing. If featured the 19th FIA World Championship, which commenced on 1 January 1968, and ended on 3 November after twelve races, and numerous non-championship races.

Graham Hill driving a Lotus 49 won the formula one championship.

Constructors Champion – Lotus Ford - The Lotus 49 was a Formula One racing car designed by Colin Chapman and Maurice Philippe for the 1967 F1 season. It was designed around the Cosworth DFV engine that would power most of the Formula One grid through the 1970s. It used its drivetrain as a stressed member, being not the first F1 car to do so, but the first to apply the technique so well that all other teams copied it.[

The 52nd International 500 Mile Sweepstakes was held at the Indianapolis Motor Speedway in Speedway, Indiana on Thursday May 30, 1968. Bobby Unser in the venerable piston-powered Offenhauser won his first of three Indy 500 victories

On September 29, 1968, Pedro Rodriguez became the first, and only to-date, Mexican driver to win the 24 Hours of Le Mans, with Lucien Bianchi in the John Wyer team's Ford GT40.

Some Programmes and tickets from 1968

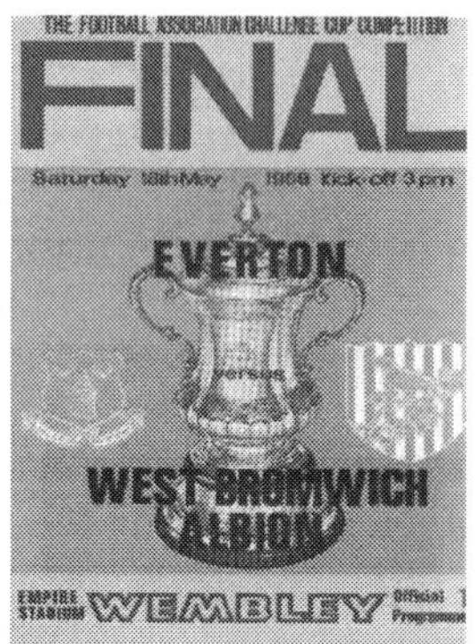

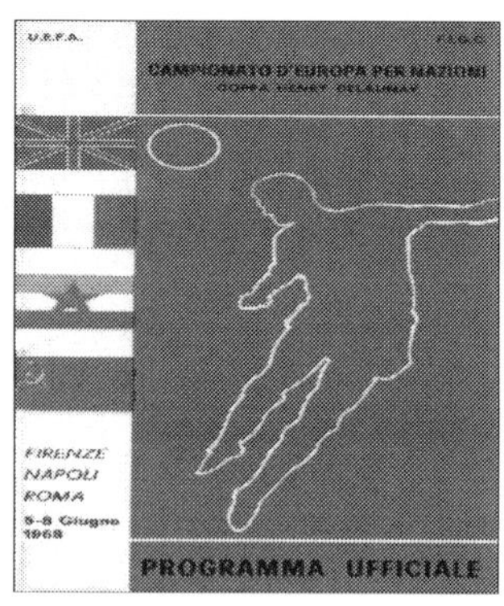

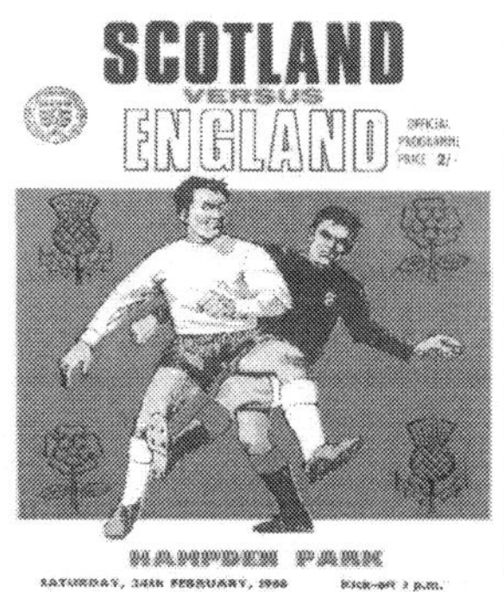

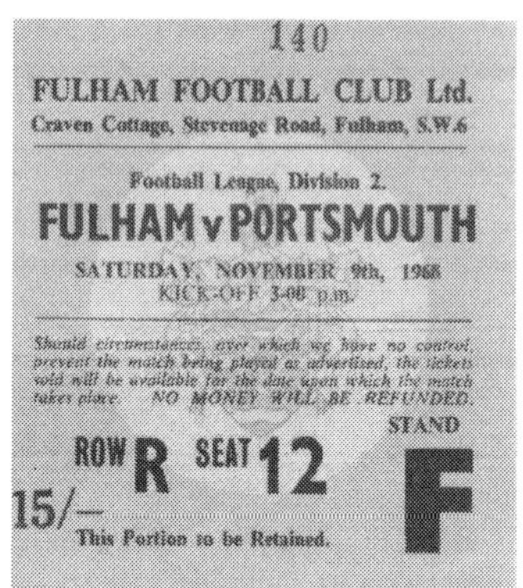

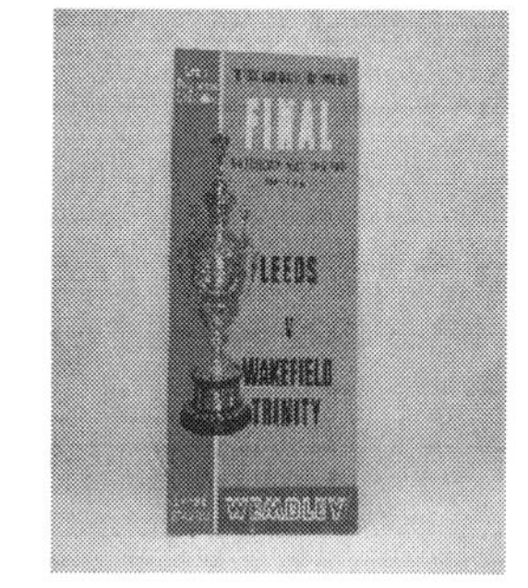

The 1968 Winter Olympics

The 1968 Winter Olympics, officially known as the X Olympic Winter Games, was celebrated in 1968 in Grenoble, France and opened on 6 February, was is the first Olympiad to adopt a mascot, although unofficially. Thirty-seven countries participated. Norway won the most medals with six gold, six silvers, and two bronzes. Frenchman Jean-Claude Killy won three gold medals in all the alpine skiing events. In women's figure skating, Peggy Fleming won the only United States gold medal. The year 1968 marked the first time the IOC first permitted East and West Germany to enter separately, and the first time the IOC ever ordered drug and gender testing of competitors. and was also the first to be broadcast in colour.

Country Medal Leaders

	Country	Gold	Silver	Bronze	Total
1	Norway	6	6	2	14
2	Soviet Union	5	5	3	13
3	Austria	3	4	4	11
4	France	4	3	2	9
5	Netherlands	3	3	3	9
6	Sweden	3	2	3	8
7	West Germany	2	2	3	7
8	United States	1	5	1	7
9	Switzerland	0	2	4	6
10	East Germany	1	2	2	5
11	Finland	1	2	2	5
12	Italy	4	0	0	4
13	Czechoslovakia	1	2	1	4
14	Canada	1	1	1	3
15	Romania	0	0	1	1

Jean-Claude Killy, won all three men's events, repeating Toni Sailer's triple-gold of 1956. Since Killy's feat, no alpine ski racer has won three gold medals in a single Olympics.

Swedish skier Toini Gustafsson was a star in women's cross-country events, winning both individual races and earning a silver medal in the relay.

American figure skater Peggy Fleming built up a huge lead after the compulsory figures and easily won the first-place votes of all nine judges.

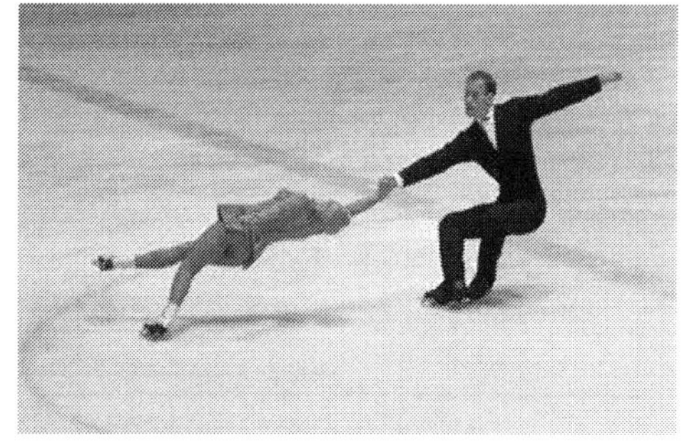

Married couple Lyudmila Belousova and Oleg Protopopov successfully defended their pairs figure skating title from Innsbruck for the Soviet Union.

Italian bobsleigh pilot Eugenio Monti drove both the two-man and four-man events to win gold.

TV RACING MIRROR

She's the Lady ..Magistrate

By NEWSBOY (Bob Butchers)

IT is eleven years since a filly won Kempton's Great Jubilee Stakes, but this run should end this afternoon (3.10).

Bright

NEWSBOY'S 'WINNER IN 3' FOR KEMPTON

3.10: Lady Magistrate, Straight Master, Chasmarella.
4.15: Massata, Golden Raisam, Marta.

KEMPTON

NEWSBOY	BOUVERIE
3.10—LADY MAGISTRATE (NAP)	3.10—TIBER
3.45—WAR LASS	3.45—WAR LASS
4.15—MASSATA	4.15—MARTA
4.45—ROYAL RUBICON	4.45—ENGLANDS GLORY

NEWSBOY'S DOUBLE: LADY MAGISTRATE and HERON'S PLUME (3.15, Newcastle).

2.0 —BENDIGO 3-Y-O H'CAP.

2.30 —SCEPTRE STAKES.

3.10 —GREAT JUBILEE H'CAP.

3.45 —MINTING 3-Y-O STAKES.

4.15 —MAYPOLE 3-Y-O FILLIES' H'CAP.

4.45 —JACK OLDING STAKES.

HAMILTON CARD

NEWSBOY	BOUVERIE
4. 0—TRENTINO	

MARKET RASEN

Selections

NEWTON ABBOT

Selections

The Perishers

COWDREY'S 148 SAVES ENGLAND

From BRIAN CHAPMAN: Port of Spain, Monday

A GREAT fighting innings of 148 by Colin Cowdrey, stoutly backed in a stand of 113 by Alan Knott, who topped fifty in his first Test of the tour, saved England from following on against West Indies here today.

Together the Kent pair retrieved batting disasters that cost the wickets of Ken Barrington, Tom Graveney and Basil D'Oliveira while only fifteen runs were added—the last two in successive balls from Rodriguez, the wily Willie of leg spin.

Knott helps his skipper with a fighting fifty

Once the skipper was out, after a magnificent and masterful display in which he hit twenty-one boundaries, another pitiful fold-up set in.

Basil Butcher, whose leg "tweekers" seldom rate a dividend, not only claimed Cowdrey's wicket but the next four as well and England were all out for 404.

When bad light ended play for the day, West Indies had made six without loss in the second innings to lead by 128 runs.

Cowdrey began as though he meant to score the needed runs off his bat.

Then, shortly after rain had held up play for thirty-five minutes at 229, Barrington, trying to lob Gibbs through his leg trap, missed and was plainly leg before.

Googly

Then came disaster! Graveney tried to cut Rodriguez and edged a catch to Deryck Murray.

D'Oliveira completely misread the Rodriguez googly, offered no stroke and was bowled first ball.

So Knott, playing in his first Test of the tour, had to fend off a hat-trick with eight men crowding round his bat.

He did so coolly enough and was soon dispersing the mantrap with rasping square cuts to the fence.

It became a joint Kent onslaught. At lunch the pair had travelled smoothly to 303 with Colin on 108.

Rain delayed the restart by half an hour, after which Colin made short work of knocking off the runs required to save the follow-on.

The stand had put on 113 in less than 160 minutes when Colin was adjudged caught at the wicket off Butcher. He was obviously surprised by umpire Sang Hue's decision after an innings which had lasted 322 minutes and included twenty-one fours.

His departure heralded a collapse, John Snow being bowled by Butcher four runs later and David Brown giving a catch at the wicket in the same over also for a duck.

Gallant

At 381 Tony Lock was leg before to Butcher's slows and 23 runs later Jeff Jones fell to the same bowler.

Knott, meanwhile, found the chance to nip to a most gallant unbeaten 69.

SCOREBOARD

WEST INDIES. — First Innings 526-7 dec. (Kanhai 153, Nurse 136, Camacho 87).

Second Innings

Camacho, not out	5
Carew, not out	1
Total (no wkt.)	6

Bowling: Brown 1-1-0-0; Snow 1-0-6-0.

ENGLAND—First Innings (Saturday 204 for 2)

Cowdrey, c Murray, b Butcher	148
Barrington, lbw, b Gibbs	48
Graveney, c Murray, b Rodriguez	8
D'Oliveira, b Rodriguez	0
Knott, not out	69
Snow, b Butcher	0
Brown, c Murray, b Butcher	0
Lock, lbw, b Butcher	3
Jones, b Butcher	1
Extras	33
Total	404

Fall of wkts: 3-245, 4-260, 5-260, 6-373, 7-377, 8-377, 9-381.

Bowling: Sobers 36-8-87-0; Gibbs 57-24-68-1; Rodriguez 35-4-145-3; Carew 25-18-23-1; Butcher 13.4-3-34-5; Griffith 3-1-7-0; Lloyd 4-2-7-0; Nurse 2-2-0-0.

CRICKET

TOUR MATCH (Singapore).—International XI 397-7 dec., Singapore 87 and 55. International XI won by an innings and 255.

PLAYBOY!

"I agree, the moon's beautiful and it's all very romantic—now shut up and let me listen to the cricket!"

LAST NIGHT'S FOOTBALL

SECOND DIVISION

Preston 2 (Ritchie, Irvine) A. Villa 1 (Greenhalgh) H.T.: 2—1 17,043

FOURTH DIVISION

Rochdale 1 (Melledew) Bradford 1 (Cockroft (o.g.)) H.T.: 0—1 1,722

Wrexham 3 (Kinsey, Moir, Smith) Chesterfield 0 H.T.: 1—0 3,000

OTHER MATCH

Arsenal 0 E. Olympic XI 3 H.T.: 0—2 (Greene (2), Davidson (og)) 3,439

IRISH F.A. CUP.—Second round, second replay: Derry 3, Glentoran 3; Portadown 3, Crusaders 4.

FOOTBALL COMBINATION.—Div. 1: Leicester 1, Chelsea 1; Div. II: Bournemouth 2, C. Palace [illegible]

SOUTHERN LEAGUE.—Premier Div.: Nuneaton 2, Hillingdon 0.

TONIGHT'S SOCCER

Kick off 7.30 unless stated

FIRST DIVISION

Nott'm F. v. Leicester

Wolverhampton v. Sheff. Wed.

SECOND DIVISION

Rotherham v. Plymouth (7.15)

THIRD DIVISION

Northampton v. Stockport

Swindon v. Shrewsbury

Watford v. Mansfield

FOURTH DIVISION

Swansea v. Southend

LAST NIGHT'S GREYHOUND RESULTS

HARRINGAY.—7.45: Knockhill Sultan [illegible] ... Guineas: [illegible]

HENDON.—7.45: Maher Abbey [illegible] 8.0: Bans Princess [illegible] 8.15: Rathbeg Lad [illegible] 8.30: Holm Treasure [illegible] 8.45: Poplar Tally [illegible] 9.0: Fleet Day [illegible] ... 9.41: New Mint Boy 4-5 f, Catherine's Chum 4-1 (1-6, 13/9). Quinela: £ 156/13/6.

WEMBLEY.—7.45: Cabby [illegible] 8.15: Marsh Kerry [illegible] 8.30: Homers [illegible] 8.36: Noel's Wonder [illegible] 8.51: Abrahan Tweed [illegible] ... Quinela: [illegible]

QUIZ-WORD

ACROSS

1. What word equals either side of the following equation? "S" + "HOOD" = "VESSEL" + "L" (5).
4. Game in which knights and bishops are pieces (5).
10. Homer's great epic poem (5).
11. Surname of the famous airwoman who disappeared without trace in 1937 (7).
12. German airship pioneer (8).
13. The "—— loris" is a kind of lemur (4).
15. Mechanical source of power (6).
17. Producer of "19" (6).
19. Alcoholic beverage (4).
20. Robber released instead of Christ by Pontius Pilate (8).
23. A breeding-place of penguins, seals etc. (7).
24. Certain good or evil spirits (5).
25. Saint associated with his brother Methodius (5).
26. What word is missing from the brackets? DAB (BEARD) HUT (TIRED) SAY (——) (5).

DOWN

2. One of the anthropoid apes, familiarly (5).
3. Wild ducks that visit Britain in winter (8).
5. Cape at the southernmost point of S. America (4).
6. Bird that catches insects on the wing (7).
7. "Mrs. ——" became the morganatic wife of the Prince of Wales, later George IV (11).
8. Northern part of the largest island of the Outer Hebrides (5).
9. That of the Chiltern Hundreds is a nominal office for an M P wishing to resign his seat (11).
14. Percussion instrument (8).
16. Pope who introduced the reformed calendar named after him (7).
18. It might mean a butterfly, an orang-utan or a very foolish person (5).
21. Forename of the man who became Prime Minister in 1922 (5).
22. "Massacre ——" defeated by Howard Winstone for the world featherweight championship (4).

YESTERDAY'S SOLUTION

ACROSS.—[illegible]

DOWN.—[illegible]

PETER WILSON

"I fear cuts may decide title fight in Duran's favour"

TWO fighters whom only their mothers could regard as being of world class, battle for the first time in Britain for the European middleweight title (11st. 11lb. 5oz.) tonight.

Wally Swift, the pride of Nottingham, and former British welter and middleweight champion, challenges Argentinian-born Italian-naturalised Juan Carlos Duran at the Embassy Sportsdrome, Birmingham.

SWIFT—IF THE EYES DON'T HAVE IT!

JUAN CARLOS DURAN
Not a big puncher.

In age there is little between them. Both are thirty-one with Duran just two months the older.

Their professional records break down as: Swift, eighty-two fights, of which he has won thirteen inside the distance, fifty-two on points, drawn three, been outpointed nine times, disqualified twice and lost inside the distance thrice.

Duran has had fifty-six fights, of which he has won forty-three, sixteen inside the distance and three on disqualifications, drawn seven, lost five, one inside the distance, and boxed one "no contest."

This is a very hard bout to sum up. Most of Duran's conquerors since he came to Europe at the end of 1960 have been top-class men.

Blot

But in the last six years he has lost only to German champion Jupp Elze and to Nino Benvenuti, the world middleweight champion.

Duran won the Italian title in July, 1966, and defended it three times before annexing the vacant European title by stopping the veteran Spanish middleweight champion, Luis Folledo, in twelve rounds.

Swift is an honest workman of the ring. He won the British welterweight title from Tommy Molloy over eight years ago but then Brian Curvis proved too good for him.

By the end of 1964, having moved up into the middleweight division he outpointed Mick Leahy for the title, only to lose it in his first defence to Johnny Pritchett.

This was one of the three times he was stopped and like the other two this was caused by the old bugbear of cuts round the eyes.

This may well be decisive tonight.

Swift fought only five times last year, losing again to Pritchett in a fight in which he suffered two facial cuts, and losing to Sandro Mazzinghi in six rounds for the European light-middleweight title, the referee having to intervene once more because of cut eyes.

If Swift can protect his vulnerable face he may well—for he is always a very fit man—outlast and outpoint the Argentinian-Italian, who is not really notable for his punching power.

But I fear that cuts may decide it in Duran's favour.

When a 'fifty-fifty' share can look rather odd

DESPITE the economic coils strangling the Government, they have certainly done their best to ensure that in an Olympic year our competitors should have more funds and facilities made available to them than ever before.

A Government grant in the region of £80,000—£20,000 more than in the 1964 Tokio games — will be available for the British Olympic Association towards the cost of sending our team to the Mexico Games in October.

Track

To enable athletes to train on the same surface as will be provided in Mexico City a £87,500 Tartan track will be provided for an eight-lane, 400 metres running track and for run-ups for the long and high jumps, pole vault and javelin.

This will be at the National Recreation Centre at Crystal Palace and the Government will meet 75 per cent. of the cost, with the remainder coming from the Greater London Council.

The Minister with special responsibilities for sport, Denis Howell, said that the total Government aid, which includes research projects into the problems associated with altitude and temperature acclimatisation training at Font Romeu in the French Pyrenees, and get-togethers of up to fourteen days for selected teams or squads in Britain, will add up to about £125,000.

In answer to a query, Howell said: "We are providing all the assurance for which we have been asked."

And he added that no one would be left out of a side whom any sports governing body thought should be selected. That, I understand, also includes coaches and trainers.

I am left with the somewhat disturbing impression that the British Olympic Association is still wedded to the idea that government aid should never be in excess of voluntary gifts of money.

Frankly I find this a rather odd state of affairs if the Government has available and is willing to provide more money than in fact has been asked for.

Burden

It certainly lays an extremely heavy burden of responsibility on the BOA for, should any legitimate performer be excluded from competition in Mexico, the question is bound to be asked whether we could not save money on the upkeep of the BOA itself now that the Government is being more forthcoming than ever before with ready cash.

I can well understand that with the ever-present fear of individual sports bodies that government money means government interference in sport, there should be a "leaning-over-backwards" attitude to ensure that no such impression is given.

But I feel that, with certain major Olympic sports in such a parlous financial plight, a harsh reappraisal of the financial situation is long overdue.

SPORT SUMMARY

BOXING

NATIONAL SPORTING CLUB [illegible]

JOHANNESBURG.—10 rnds. light-heavy: Sakkie Pieterse (S. Africa) outpts. Ernie Field (U.S.)

GOLF

FLORIDA CITRUS OPEN TOURNAMENT (Orlando).—Final leading scores: [illegible]

CINEMAS

ASTORIA, Char. X-rd. Tommy Steele in HALF A SIXPENCE (U). [illegible]

COLUMBIA [illegible] Spencer Tracy, Katharine Hepburn, Sidney Poitier, GUESS WHO'S COMING TO DINNER [illegible]

DOMINION [illegible] THE SOUND OF MUSIC [illegible]

LEIC. SQ. TH. [illegible] CAROLYN ON DOCTOR [illegible]

METROPOLE [illegible] FAR FROM THE MADDING CROWD [illegible]

ODEON Haymarket [illegible] A Man For All Seasons [illegible]

ODEON Leic. Square [illegible]

ODEON Marble Arch [illegible]

ODEON St. Martin's Lane [illegible] DOCTOR DOLITTLE [illegible]

Sporting Events in 1968

January

10th Tottenham Hotspur manager, Bill Nicholson signed Martin Chivers (photo's below) for a club record fee of £125,000, which also made him the country's most expensive player at that time.

12th-21st The 6th edition of the African Cup of Nations was played in Ethiopia when the field was expanded to eight teams, split into two groups of four; the top two teams in each group advanced to the semifinals. Congo-Kinshasa won its first championship, beating Ghana in the final 1–0. Prior to this tournament, the African Cup of Nations were held once every three years, following 1968 they were held once every two years.

13th On this day, the pools were cancelled for this day due to a big freeze when many games were postponed, at least 31 games were cancelled.

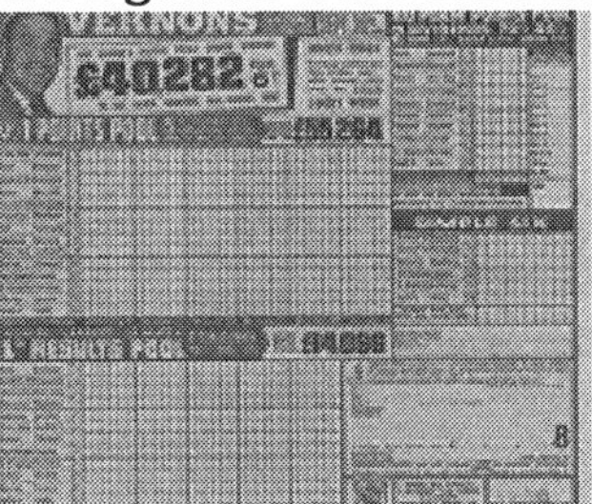

13th Start of the Rugby Five Nations when France beat Scotland 8 – 6

19th The 1968 Wimbledon tennis championships were the first edition of the tournament to offer prize money. The total prize money for the event was £26,150. The winner of the men's title earned £2,000 while the women's singles champion earned £750. First round losers were £50 for men £25 pounds for ladies

19th – 24th Start of the test series in the West Indies, which ended in a draw after England scored 568, West Indies scored 363 and 243 for eight

20th England v Wales in the five nations, it finished 11 - 11

24th Howard Winstone (photo below) fought the Japanese boxer, Mitsunori Seki for the vacant WBC world featherweight title at the Royal Albert Hall. He won when the fight was stopped in the ninth due to a cut eye, and so finally gained a world title.
In July 1968, he defended his world title against the Cuban, Jose Legra. But unfortunately, he sustained a badly swollen left eye, which caused the bout to be stopped in the fifth round. Winstone decided to retire at the age of 29.

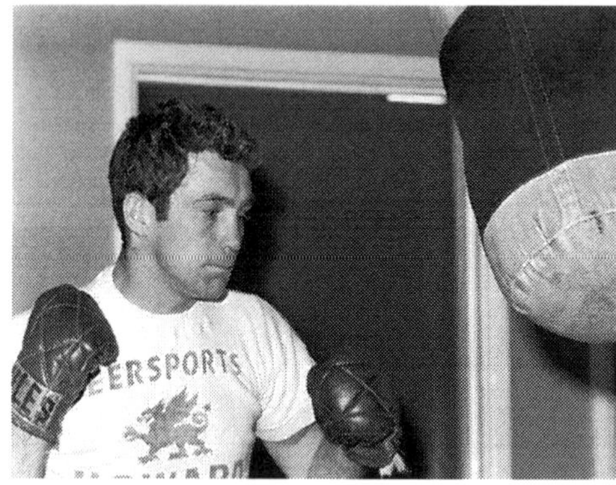

27th France v Ireland in the five nations 16 – 5

February

6th – 18th The Winter Games in Grenoble, France started, Jean-Claude Killy from the host country captured the world's attention when he won three gold medals in Alpine skiing. Peggy Fleming, age 19, won a gold medal in figure skating for the United States. East Germany and West Germany competed separately for the first time.
It was an Olympic Winter Games full of firsts. Host nation France witnessed the introduction of the gender test for women, doping controls for all athletes and was also the first to be broadcast in colour. Norway finished top of the leader board with 14 medals, including six golds.

8th – 14th 2nd test v. West Indies, which ended in a draw, when escaped defeat by two minutes and two wickets, when under a lot of pressure.

24th Scotland v England drew 1 – 1 in nation cup match in front of a crowd of 134,000. John Hughes scored for Scotland and Martin Peter for England

28th Manchester United beat Gornik Zabrze in the first leg of their European cup first leg tie

29th West Indies and England had another draw in their 3rd test match

March

2nd The 1968 Football League Cup Final took place on 2 March 1968 at Wembley Stadium. It was the eighth final and the second to be played at Wembley. It was contested between Arsenal and Leeds United. Terry Cooper scored the only goal of the game with an attendance of 97,887

6th Europe Cup Winners Quarter Final Cardiff v Torpedo Moscow, 1 – 0

14th – 19th 4th Test, West Indies v England at Port of Spain, which was won by England 7 wickets, giving them a 1 – 0 lead in the series

19th Europe Cup Winners Quarter Final Torpedo Moscow v Cardiff 1 – 0, the game then went to reply which Cardiff won 1 – 0

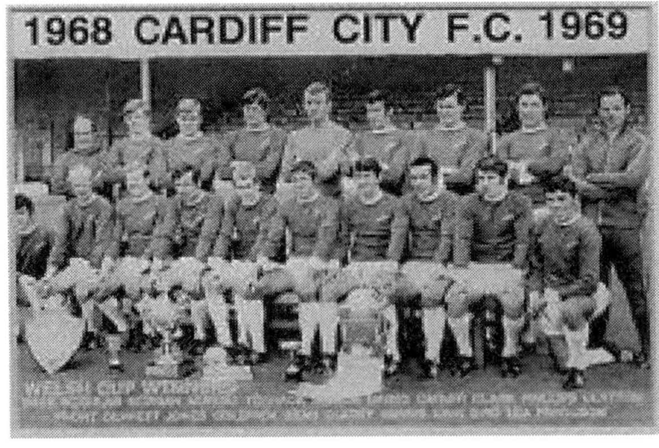

Mar 28th - Apr 3rd Fifth and final test West Indies and England, giving England, a series win.

30th The 1968 Grand National was the 122nd renewal of the world-famous Grand National horse race that took place at. The winner was the nine-year-old Red Alligator, by 20 lengths. He was ridden by jockey Brian Fletcher, who later rode Red Rum to victory in 1973 and 1974.

APRIL

7th James Clark, Jr OBE (4 March 1936 – 7 April 1968), known as Jim Clark, was a British Formula One racing driver from Scotland, who won two World Championships, in 1963 and 1965.
He was killed in a Formula Two motor racing accident in Hockenheim, Germany in 1968.

11th - 14th The 1968 Masters Tournament was the 32nd Masters Tournament, held at Augusta National Golf Club in Augusta, Georgia. Bob Goalby won his only major championship, one stroke ahead of Roberto DeVicenzo. At first it appeared that he had tied DeVicenzo and the two would meet in an 18-hole Monday playoff, but DeVicenzo returned an incorrect scorecard showing a par 4 on the 17th hole, instead of a birdie 3, sunk with a two-foot putt. Playing partner Tommy Aaron incorrectly marked the 4 and DeVicenzo failed to catch the mistake and signed the scorecard.

19th - 21st The 1st European Badminton Championships were held in Bochum (Germany). Sweden's Sture Johnsson (photo below) won the gold medal in the singles and the German Irmgard Latz won the gold medal in the ladies singles. While the English pairs David Eddy and Roger Powell won the men's doubles, Margaret Boxall and Susan Whetnall (photo below), won the women doubles and Tony Jordan and Susan Whetnall won the mixed double's

24th 1st leg of the European Cup Winners Cup Hamburg v Cardiff finished 1 -1

25th The 20th BRDC International Trophy was a non-championship Formula One race was held over 52 laps of the Silverstone circuit. Denny Hulme won, driving a McLaren-Cosworth M7A. Bruce McLaren 3rd was Chris Amon, giving New Zealand a podium lock-out. With the second Ferrari in fourth, driven by Jacky Ickx, the first English driver home was Piers Courage in his privately entered BRM P126.

May

1st Second leg of the European Cup Winners Cup - Cardiff v Hamburg finished 3 -2 to Hamburg, losing 4 -3 on aggregate.

13th Walter McGowan lost his British and Commonwealth bantamweight titles at Belle Vue, Manchester. to Alan Rudkin in a fifteen-round points decision.

RUDKIN GETS HIS REVENGE IN A GREAT, BITTER BATTLE

PETER WILSON reports 'an old-fashioned fighting evening'

But brave McGowan is so close to keeping his titles in storming finish

WE PLAY SAYS MIKE—AND EARNS £3,700

ASHMAN PUTS BAN ON CUP PERKS

SPORT SUMMARY

AMUSEMENTS AND ENTERTAINMENTS

specify Ruberoid roofings

18th The FA Cup played at Wembley West Bromwich Albion v Everton. Jeff Astle scored the game's only goal in the third minute of extra-time to win the match. It was the first FA Cup final to be shown in colour.

29th The 1968 European Cup Final between Benfica of Portugal and Manchester United of England, at Wembley Stadium with Manchester United winning 4–1 after extra time.

JUNE

5th – 10th The 1968 UEFA European Football Championship final tournament was held in Italy. It was in this year that the tournament changed its name from the European Nations' Cup to the European Championship.

There were also some changes in the tournament's qualifying structure, with the two-legged home-and-away knock-out stage being replaced by a group phase.

Only four countries played in the final tournament. Italy, Soviet Union Yugoslavia and England. Italy the host country beat Yugoslavia after a reply, England won the third place play off.

5th Alan Mullery became the first the first player ever to be sent off in a full England international match, he was given his marching orders for a retaliatory tackle on Yugoslavian player Dobrivoje Trivić.

LONELY WALK INTO SOCCER HISTORY

Sent off . . . and this time the walk is lonelier than ever because Alan Mullery is the first England player sent off in a full international. He was involved in a clash just two minutes before the end of a sad England match.

EXIT ENGLAND—IN SHAME

Mullery sent off as they crash to last-gasp goal

'You can kick a player in front of ref..'

PANCHO WINS—AS EMMO RUNS OUT OF GAS

6th - 11th

Australia won the first test vs England in Manchester by 159 runs.

May 27th - June 9th

The 1968 French Open Tennis Tournament at the Stade Roland Garros in Paris, France It was the first Grand Slam that allowed professional players, marking the beginning of the tennis Open Era, which continues to the present day. Second-seeded Ken Rosewall won the final 6–3, 6–1, 2–6, 6–2 against first-seeded Rod Laver.

Nancy Richey defeated Ann Jones 5–7, 6–4, 6–1 in the final to win the Women's Singles tennis title.

Ken Rosewall (photo below) and Fred Stolle defeated Roy Emerson and Rod Laver 6–3, 6–4, 6–3 in the final to win the Men's Doubles title.

The second-seeded team of Françoise Dürr and Ann Jones won the title, defeating the first-seeded pair of Rosie Casals and Billie Jean King in the final in three sets.

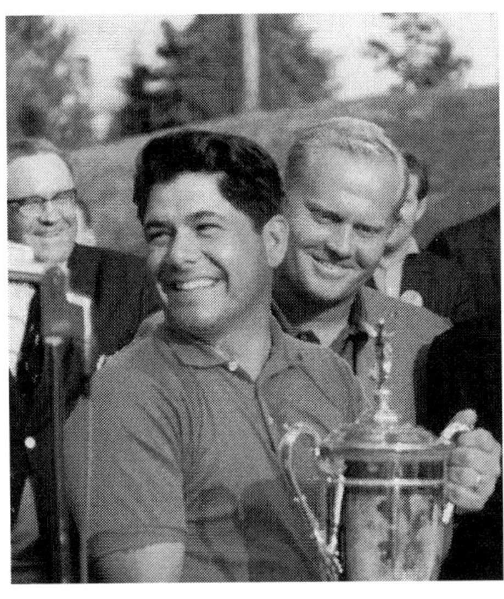

13th –16th

The 1968 U.S. Open was the 68th U.S. Open, held at the East Course of Oak Hill Country Club in Rochester, New York.

Lee Trevino (photo above) equaled the tournament scoring record and won the first of his six major titles, four strokes ahead of runner-up Jack Nicklaus. It was also the first win on the PGA Tour for Trevino, age 28.

20th –24th

The 1968 LPGA Championship was the held at Pleasant Valley Country Club in Sutton, Massachusetts, southeast of Worcester. In an 18-hole Monday playoff, Sandra Post won her only major title, defeating defending champion Kathy Whitworth by seven strokes. Post turned 20 earlier in the month and this was the first of her eight victories on the LPGA Tour.

20th - 25th 2nd Test at Lords between Australia v England, the match was a draw.

24th - 6th July This tournament started the open era for Wimbledon, as it became the second Grand Slam tournament to offer prize money and allow professionals to compete after the 1968 French Open. In the men final Rod Laver beat fellow Australian Tony Roche, 6–3, 6–4, 6–2.
While in ladies final, America Billie Jean King defeated Australia Judy Tegart, 9–7, 7–5
In the men's doubles, it was a an all Australian final when John Newcombe / Tony Roche defeated Ken Rosewall / Fred Stolle, 3–6, 8–6, 5–7, 14–12, 6–3
In the Ladies doubles the US pair Rosemary Casals / Billie Jean King defeated the couple, Françoise Dürr from France and the English lady Ann Jones, 3–6, 6–4, 7–5

PAGE 22 DAILY MIRROR, Saturday, July 6, 1968

Murder in a green cathedral

LAVER UNDISPUTED CHAMPION OF WORLD TENNIS

ROD LAVER'S 6–3, 6–4, 6–2 victory over Tony Roche in the men's final at Wimbledon yesterday was murder in green cathedral.

Not since Lew Hoad's second win against Ashley Cooper in 1957 has there been such a formidable steamrollering of the opposition by a great champion ... unless it was Laver's own second win as an amateur against Martin Mulligan six years ago.

PETER WILSON reporting from Wimbledon

Genius

Ease

Vital

Nervous

Rod Laver's finest hour has a few minutes to run by the Centre Court clock before he is declared undisputed champion of the world at Wimbledon yesterday.

Scots hang on to title

NEW LION WEST WON'T GET MUCH REST

By MIRROR SPORT REPORTER

SPORT SUMMARY

Today on Centre Court

But in the doubles..Roche wins and Laver loses

By C M JONES

COLDWELL PLAYS

July

11th -16th — 3rd Test Australia v England match drawn at Edgbaston

10th - 13th — The 1968 Open Championship was the 97th Open Championship, played at Carnoustie Golf Links. Gary Player won the second of his three Open titles, two strokes ahead of runners-up Bob Charles and Jack Nicklaus. It was the fifth of Player's nine major titles.

BOB RODNEY, WHO PICKED THE OPEN WINNER FROM A FIELD OF 130 STARTERS, SAYS:

Gary plays a blinder and leaves them all cold

PLAYER AT 9-1 BEST BET IN 'OPEN'

NEW SWING CLICKS FOR BEMBRIDGE

Success

Toughest

CROSSWORD

LANCASHIRE LOSE GRIP

By HOWARD BOOTH

CRICKET SCOREBOARD

Large family outing for a £250 prize

GIBSON CARRIES CAN FOR DEFEAT

SPOT ON—AND CARD

NIGHT RACING

Safe

AMUSEMENTS

18th -21st — The 1968 PGA Championship was the 50th PGA Championship played at Pecan Valley Golf Club in San Antonio, Texas. Julius Boros, (photo below) age 48, won the third of his three major titles, one stroke ahead of runners-up Bob Charles and Arnold Palmer. Boros remains the oldest winner of a major championship.

24th Howard Winstone defended his newly won world title against the Cuban, Jose Legra, at Porthcawl, Wales. He was knocked down twice in the first round. He continued fighting, but unfortunately, he sustained a badly swollen left eye, which caused the bout to be stopped in the fifth round. Having lost the world title in his first defense, Winstone decided to retire at the age of 29.

25th – 30th 4th Test Australia v England match drawn at Headingley Leeds

August

7th First leg of the Inter-Cites Fairs Cup, when Leeds beat Ferencvaros 1 – 0 with Mick Jones scoring the only goal.

DAILY MIRROR, Thursday, August 8, 1968 PAGE 23

Leeds one goal up . . but Cup trouble looms in Budapest

OLD FEAR HAUNTS REVIE MEN

By KEN JONES

THE reputation of Ferencvaros as a team of glowing quality was lost last night as they succumbed to the cynicism of European football.

For Leeds, on the threshold of a season when they have promised to play with more ambition, it was a frustrating experience.

FAIRS CUP FINAL (First leg)	
LEEDS	1
FERENCVAROS	0

Industry

Freshness

PLAYBOY!

"You can speak Hungarian, Fred— tell that big twit to take a running jump at himself!"

Bobby Charlton sticks his neck out

BOBBY CHARLTON, of Manchester United and England, so often acclaimed as the world's most popular footballer, takes on the risky role of prophet in the first issue of Goal, the colourful and exciting new Soccer weekly.

In the "Bobby Charlton Diary," which he will write in Goal every week, he says:

Of EVERTON:

"They are one of the youngest teams, but the line-up is packed with skill. And for all their lack of years they can produce experience where it is needed most—from Ray Wilson, Brian Labone and Gordon West in defence and from Alan Ball up front."

And of WEST BROMWICH ALBION . . .

"Now that Albion have won the Cup and tasted success, they'll be looking to win something again this season. They've broken the psychological barrier, proving themselves to themselves, so they could be a considerable force."

Charlton goes on . . .

"I want to stick my neck out a bit and give a couple of outsiders—West Ham and Sunderland. If I lived and played in London I'd be livid at the way the southern teams get written off each year. The pride of the lads down there must be hurt, so I think we'll see a very strong challenge from them.

"Spurs are always hard to beat, and I think Chelsea will do well with Dave Sexton at the helm. But I'll stick with the Hammers . . . they'll take a lot of stopping. There's certainly nothing wrong with their attack."

Oxford plan 1970 move to £100,000 stadium

By NIGEL CLARKE

OXFORD UNITED, newcomers to the Second Division, plan to quit their homely little ground at Manor Road—for a £100,000 super stadium two miles down the road.

QUIZ-WORD

ACROSS

DOWN

YESTERDAY'S SOLUTION

10th — Start of the Football season

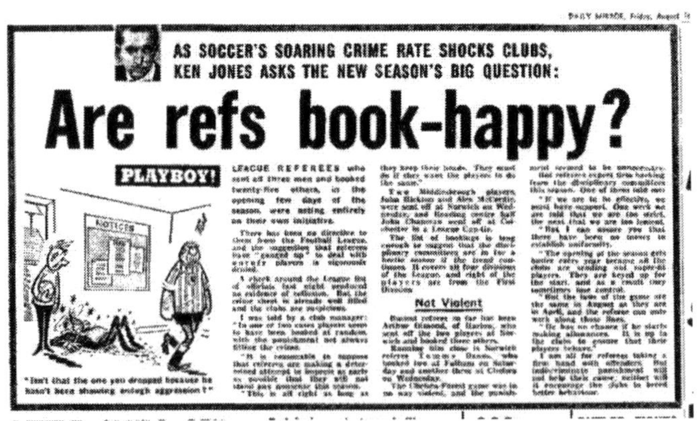

AS SOCCER'S SOARING CRIME RATE SHOCKS CLUBS, KEN JONES ASKS THE NEW SEASON'S BIG QUESTION:

Are refs book-happy?

PLAYBOY!

Not Violent

29th - 8th September. — The 1968 US Open took place at the West Side Tennis Club, Forest Hills in New York, It was the 88th staging of the tournament and the fourth Grand Slam event of 1968. It was the first edition of the tournament in the Open Era of tennis and as such for the first time offered prize money, totaling $100,000. Arthur Ashe and Virginia Wade (photo's below) won the singles titles. Ashe was still registered as an amateur and therefore not entitled to the $14,000 first-prize money, which instead went to runner-up Tom Okker, while Wade earned $6,000.

22th - 27th — 5th Test Australia v England at Oval, England won by 226 runs. Meaning the series was a draw 1 - 1

29th — Basil D'Oliveira was left out of tour to South Africa

September

11th — On a night of immense tension, Leeds United were subjected to their most rigorous European examination in the white-hot atmosphere of the Nep Stadium, becoming the first British winners of the Inter-Cities Fairs Cup drawing with Ferencvaros 0 - 0.

Exactly a week later United started the defense of their new trophy as they travelled to Belgium to face Standard Liege!

12th First leg of the 1968–69 European Cup Winners' Cup Club Bruges v West Bromwich Albian, it finished 3–1 to Bruges, when three players was sent off, West Bromwich went to win 2–0 at home, 3-3 on aggregate. West Brom went out in quarter final losing to Dunfermline Athletic

POLICE CHARGE ON TO THE PITCH TO BREAK UP BIG CUP BATTLE

Astle is rushed to hospital as players riot

By PETER INGALL: Bruges 3, West Bromwich Albion 1

JEFF ASTLE, scorer of West Bromwich Albion's F A Cup-winner's goal, was taken unconscious to hospital with severe concussion following a goalmouth riot in this European Cup-winners' Cup first-round clash in Bruges last night.

Spectators Join In

FOUR SENT OFF IN LEAGUE FLARE-UPS

SPEEDWAY

CINEMAS

Misery

Striker Alan Birchenall soars above a line of white-shirted Morton defenders to head Chelsea's second goal in last night's Fairs Cup-tie at Stamford Bridge.

MERCILESS CHELSEA WIN IN A CANTER

By KEN JONES

Chelsea 5, Morton 0

SCOTLAND'S Morton found last night that Chelsea are as uncharitable as the best of the teams in their own country.

Took Control

Faded

TROUBLE NIGHT IN EUROPE FOR BRITISH TEAMS

By HARRY MILLER

Hit Back

£100,000 HATELEY MAY MOVE TODAY

Results, scorers

Super Seymour saves Fulham hammering

LONGSIGHT'S FIXED ODDS HINTS

18th Karl Mildenberger's career ended when he lost the European Heavyweight title to Henry Cooper when he was disqualified in the eighth round

KING OF EUROPE AGAIN!

Cooper gets a cut eye but German is ruled out in a mixed-up finish

Karl's manager will lodge an official protest

HENRY COOPER achieved his great ambition at Wembley last night when he won the European heavyweight title from Karl Mildenberger just two seconds before the end of the eighth round.

PETER WILSON reporting from the ringside at Wembley

Signal

Warning

Whipped

QUIZ-WORD

SPORTS SUMMARY

ORDER GOAL TODAY

MANCHESTER UNITED—WORLD CLUB CHAMPIONS?

17th John Vorster, South Africa Premier, put a ban on Basil D'Oliveira coming to South Africa on the MCC tour after he was included after Tom Cartwright withdrawn from the tour with injury. Mr. Vorster denounced his selection and said, "It is the team of the anti-apartheid movement". The tour was called off later in the month.

Daily Mirror

Wednesday, September 18, 1968

"We are not prepared to receive a team thrust upon us by.. political foes"

VORSTER PUTS BAN ON DOLLY

THE MCC tour of South Africa is almost certainly off.

South Africa's Premier John Vorster last night uncompromisingly banned any team that includes Cape Coloured cricketer Basil D'Oliveira.

And MCC secretary Billy Griffith declared: "If the chosen team is not acceptable to South Africa, the whole thing will be called off."

Now it looks as though the tour is off

Dismay

EXPORTS SMASH RECORDS

Hopes of cut in Bank Rate as the £ gets a boost

Open

October

10th – 12th 1968 Piccadilly World Match Play Championship was the fifth World Match Play Championship.
Eight players competed in a straight knock-out competition, with each match contested over 36 holes. The champion received £5,000 out of a total prize fund of £16,000. The runner up received £3,000, losing semi-finalists £2,000 and the first round losers £1,000, In the final Gary Player beat Bob Charles at the 36th hole to win the tournament for the third time in four years.
The tournament included two British golfers: Brian Huggett and Tony Jacklin.

12th – 27th The Mexico Summer Olympics with 112 countries taking part with 5516 competitors taking part in 172 events

16th During the Olympics Tommie Smith & John Carlos give a black power salute

18th Bob Beamon of USA sets long jump record (29 ft. 2½ in.) in Mexico City

25th Longest Olympic field hockey game took place in Mexico The Netherlands beats Spain 1-0 in 2h25m, going into ten overtimes.

November

3rd The 1968 Formula One season was the 22nd season of the FIA's Formula One motor racing. The championship was won by Graham Hill winning the last race in Mexico, to win the championship by 12 points, Jackie Stewart.

4th – 13th The 1968 Summer Paralympics this was the third Paralympic Games to be held. The games were originally planned to be held alongside the 1968 Summer Olympics in Mexico City, but in 1966, the Mexican government decided against it due to difficulties. The Israeli government offered to host the games in Tel Aviv, a suggestion that was accepted.
The United States topped the table with 99 medals Great Britain 2nd and Israel 3rd

"Hope you're picking up some good tips —I'm taking you Christmas shopping next week!"

December

5th Tommy Docherty left his job with Queen Park Rangers after 28 days after a disagreement with the chairman about signing a playing, he joined Aston Villa 13 days later.

In 1968, hurdler David Hemery was named Sports Personality of the Year.

Hemery won the 400m hurdles at that year's Olympic Games in Mexico, setting a world record time of 48.12 seconds.

Top team boss admits it—'we must be only second favourites'

I FEAR MATT SAYS MERCER

MANCHESTER CITY arrive at their Tottenham Corner today in a First Division championship chase tight enough to make the Derby look tame.

Last night manager Joe Mercer looked at today's key clash at White Hart-lane and said: "If we come out of this one still at the top of the table we'll take some stopping."

By HARRY MILLER

All Manchester sees the race as a one-city, two-club photo-finish . . . with Mercer candidly commenting: "We must be second favourites to United."

Both clubs have two games to go—United's are at home, City's away. They have the same points but City have the better goal average.

Congestion

Both clubs should be looking over their shoulders at Leeds, who are hit by fixture congestion, but only a point behind and with a game in hand.

The battle between City and United is being directed by managers who are friends and neighbours.

Mercer, with that wonderfully warm grin, explains: "Matt Busby and I . . . we live just a hundred yards away from each other.

"We've been trying to fix up a game of golf for the past month. But we just can't seem to get together.

"Still, I expect I'll see Matt if we carry off that pot—I'll have to go over the road to Old Trafford to collect it.

"We know it isn't going to be easy at Tottenham. They're a fine side. But we will be going out to attack. After all, a win is the only result that will keep us going."

United are home to Newcastle and Leeds are home to Liverpool. Both have injury problems.

Nobby Stiles and Denis Law are out of United's match. Veteran Bill Foulkes is recalled at centre half and David Sadler switches to Stiles' spot.

Leeds' cause has not been helped by the Football League refusing them a postponement of their game at Arsenal next Tuesday.

Doubts

Or by fitness doubts concerning Jackie Charlton and Mick Jones.

Who goes down with Fulham? The odds and the remaining fixtures suggest it will be Coventry or Sheffield United.

But if Coventry can win at West Ham today and Sheffield fail at Burnley, it will look bleak for the Yorkshiremen.

Who takes over from the drop-outs? Ipswich, with a doubt over talented Danny Hegan's fitness, can clinch their place by winning at Portsmouth.

That task should not be beyond a side unbeaten in thirteen games.

Queen's Park Rangers have to beat Birmingham at home to stay in front of Blackpool.

Rangers must — and should—win.

HOPE GOES ON THE LIST OF CUP CROCKS

By PETER INGALL

BOBBY HOPE is the latest member of West Brom's Cup Final squad to go on the injury list. He has a strained hip.

Hope plus left back Graham Williams and right back Tony Brown miss today's game at Sunderland.

Skipper Williams is still troubled by a knee strain. Brown has an injured thigh and ankle.

None of the injuries is serious, and there was more cheer for manager Alan Ashman yesterday.

Wing half Doug Fraser and left winger Clive Clark are recovered from injuries received in the great 6—3 win over Manchester United and play today.

Wolves go out at Molineux against Chelsea today chasing the two points they need to stay in the First Division.

Manager Ronnie Allen said: "Two more points will do because our goal average is so good it is worth another point."

Torquay hopes go crashing

Scunthorpe 2, Torquay 0

TORQUAY crashed to a shock defeat against a team already bound for Division Four—and now their promotion hopes are desperately weak.

Scunthorpe didn't look like a team in trouble, but Torquay still had enough chances to win convincingly.

Centre forward Graham Rusling hit the first goal after 32 minutes, after 'keeper Andy Donnelly had made two fine saves.

Left half Mel Blyth scored No. 2 with twelve minutes to go.

STILES MISSES MADRID TRIP

MANCHESTER UNITED'S Nobby Stiles has withdrawn from the England party to travel to Madrid for Wednesday's Nations' Cup quarter-final, owing to a knee injury.

England manager Alf Ramsey has added Everton's Brian Labone to his squad because of doubts about Jackie Charlton of Leeds.

The England Under-23 match against Germany has been switched from June 2 to June 3. Other games on the tour are in Italy and Hungary.

PLAYBOY!

"I don't care if you HAVE had yer innings—you should stay till the end like everybody else!"

TIMID M C C LEAVE TOO MUCH TO SKIPPER MILTON

By PETER LAKER

THE TAME batsmen of M C C did nothing to promote the cause of brighter cricket in settling for a draw against Surrey at Lord's yesterday apart from Gloucestershire veteran Arthur Milton.

By chance—or ill chance—skipper Milton had to open in place of Mike Denness, who had two stitches in a nose gash after colliding with the boundary fence near the close of the Surrey innings.

With 203 in 190 minutes the target, the 40-year-old Milton, whose 2,089 runs topped the scoring charts last season, dictated with a sound technique that put victory well within M C C's compass.

He scored 69, mainly off the back foot, in 140 minutes, but the innings was always lacking in enterprise at the other end.

And once Milton departed, lbw to seamer Stewart Storey at 117 for three, the ship gently cruised to 137-7 ten minutes into "extra time."

Boredom

A loudspeaker announcement reminded the crowd of the new rule calling for twenty overs in the last hour, and told us that there were eight overs left.

Denness, reappearing at No. 6, piloted M C C to 137 without further mishap, but with little relief to the boredom.

England offspinner Pat Pocock joins Milton on the honours list as the player who contributed most.

He hit a bright unbeaten 39 (five 4s) in a last-wicket stand of 47 in thirty minutes with Robin Harman (17)—a bonus that helped Surrey to 133. Then he followed with a tidy 24-over spell to take four for 52.

TODAY'S CRICKET

[illegible]

GILLETTE CUP
(First Round)

[illegible]

SCOREBOARD

LORDS.—M C C drew with Surrey. [illegible] M C C 137-7 [illegible] (Milton 69; Pocock 4 for 52).

OXFORD.—Oxford Univ. drew with Warwickshire. [illegible]

HOVE.—Sussex (5 pts.) drew with Hampshire (2 pts.). [illegible]

DERBY.—Derbyshire [illegible] drew with Middlesex [illegible] Abandoned rain.

CAMBRIDGE.—Yorkshire beat Cambridge Univ. [illegible]

SPORTS SUMMARY

THIRD DIVISION

Scunthorpe 2 Torquay 0

Southport 0 Grimsby 0

Top positions

[illegible]

FOOTBALL COMBINATION.—[illegible]

SOUTHERN LEAGUE.—[illegible] Canterbury 3, Tonbridge 1.

NORTH MIDLAND LEAGUE.—Doncaster 4, Bradford 2.

KENT FLOODLIGHT CUP.—Margate 5, Gravesend 2.

LAWN TENNIS

LONDON HARD COURTS LAWN TENNIS CHAMPIONSHIPS [illegible]

DAVIS CUP [illegible]

GOLF

HOUSTON CHAMPIONS TOURNAMENT [illegible]

£4,000 PENFOLD PRO TOURNAMENT [illegible]

SPEEDWAY

CHALLENGE MATCH.—[illegible]

CHALLENGE MATCH.—[illegible]

BRITISH LEAGUE.—[illegible]

CONFIDENT HORTON SNATCHES THE LEAD

By BOB RODNEY

TOMMY HORTON, 26, threw off his inferiority complex and grabbed a one-stroke lead in the £4,000 Penfold tournament at Maesdu, Llandudno yesterday.

After a two-under-par 71, for a halfway total of 140, Horton said: "People told me I didn't hit the ball far enough and I've always worried about distance, because I'm small.

"But when I played in the US Masters in America at Easter I found I was out-driving the stars like Billy Casper and Doug Sanders.

"Now, I'm confident with my two wood and two iron and if this wind keeps up, it will improve my chances."

An accurate two wood second at the fourth, helped him to his first birdie, a four.

Powerful

Then a long drive at the eighth followed by a fine chip with a sand iron, set up the second.

Powerful blows with the two iron and two wood at the long par four holes of the inward half helped him beat par by two shots.

Tommy Halpin, 20-year-old Irishman, who broke the course record on Thursday, had a 74, and is second on 141.

He three-putted three times and said: "That's most unusual for me."

His partner, Cyril Pennington, went out of bounds at the ninth and took a seven, but he chipped into the hole at the 14th for a birdie three, and finished with 74 for 142.

Joint third on 142 is last year's winner John Cockin. He dropped two shots in the first three holes, then hit back with five birdies in a round of 70.

He said: "I'm a new man, so calm and cool. Last year if I'd started like that I would have taken 80."

TEST CASH ROLLS IN

Yorkshire have taken £18,000 in advance ticket bookings for the Headingley Test against Australia starting on July 25.

POOLS CHECK

3.0 kick-off unless otherwise stated.

First Division

Burnley v. Sheff. Utd.
Everton v. Stoke
Fulham v. Southampton
Leeds v. Liverpool
Leicester v. Nottm. For.
Man. Utd. v. Newcastle
Sheff. Wed. v. Arsenal
Sunderland v. W.B.A.
Tottenham v. Man. City
West Ham v. Coventry
Wolverhampton v. Chelsea

Second Division

Aston Villa v. Bristol City
Cardiff v. Huddersfield
Charlton v. Hull
C. Palace v. Middlesbrough
Derby v. Blackpool
Norwich v. Carlisle
Plymouth v. Bolton
Portsmouth v. Ipswich
Preston v. Millwall
Q.P.R. v. Birmingham (3.15)
Rotherham v. Blackburn

Third Division

Barrow v. Shrewsbury
Bournemouth v. Tranmere
Bristol Rov. v. Swindon
Bury v. Stockport (3.15)
Colchester v. Orient
Mansfield v. Walsall (3.15)
Oldham v. Reading (3.15)
Oxford Utd. v. Brighton
Peterborough v. Northampton
Watford v. Gillingham

Fourth Division

Aldershot v. York
Brad. City v. Doncaster
Chester v. Barnsley (3.15)
Chesterfield v. Swansea (3.15)
Crewe v. Luton
Darlington v. Newport (3.15)
Exeter v. Hartlepools
Halifax v. Bradford
Lincoln v. Brentford (7.15)
Notts. Co. v. Southend
Port Vale v. Wrexham (3.15)
Workington v. Rochdale

Southern League Premier Division

Barnet v. Yeovil
Cambridge City v. Romford
Dover v. Wellington
[illegible] v. King's Lynn
Hereford v. Cambridge Utd.
Hillingdon v. Corby
Margate v. Poole
Nuneaton v. Burton
Stevenage v. Cheltenham
Weymouth v. Guildford
Wimbledon v. Chelmsford

The 1968 Summer Olympics

The 1968 Summer Olympics were held in Mexico City, Mexico, in October 1968.
These were the first Olympic Games to be staged in Latin America and the first to be staged in a Spanish-speaking country. They were also the first Games to use an all-weather (smooth) track for track and field events instead of the traditional cinder track.
It was the first Olympic games in which the closing ceremony was transmitted in color to the world, as well as the events themselves

Rank	Country	Gold	Sliver	Bronze	Total
1	United States	45	28	34	107
2	Soviet Union	29	32	30	91
3	Japan	11	7	7	25
4	Hungary	10	10	12	32
5	East Germany	9	9	7	25
6	France	7	3	5	15
7	Czechoslovakia	7	2	4	13
8	West Germany	5	11	10	26
9	Australia	5	7	5	17
10	Great Britain	5	5	3	13
15	Mexico (host nation)	3	3	3	9

British Medalists

Gold

David Hemery — Athletics, Men's 400m Hurdles

Chris Finnegan — Boxing, Men's Middleweight

Derek Allhusen, Jane Bullen, Ben Jones, and Richard Meade
Equestrian, Three-Day Event Team Competition

Bob Braithwaite — Shooting, Men's Trap Shooting

Rodney Pattisson & Iain MacDonald-Smith — Sailing, Men's Flying Dutchman

Silver

Lillian Board — Athletics, Women's 400 metres

Sheila Sherwood — Athletics, Women's Long Jump

Derek Allhusen — Equestrian, Three-Day Event Individual Competition

Marion Coakes — Equestrian, Jumping Individual Competition

Martyn Woodroffe — Swimming, Men's 200m Butterfly

Bronze

John Sherwood — Athletics, Men's 400m Hurdles

David Broome — Equestrian, Jumping Individual Competition

Robin Aisher, Paul Anderson, and Adrian Jardine — Sailing, Men's 5½ Meter Class

British winners at Olympics

David Hemery won the 400m hurdles in 48.12 seconds, a new world record. In the final, he took the race out hard. By the final straight, he had an ever-growing lead over the world record holder Geoff Vanderstock. Hemery continued to pour it on, taking seven tenths of a second out of the world record,

Fighting in the middleweight division, Chris Finnegan's beat Aleksei Kiselyov of the Soviet Union in the final to win the gold medal.

Bob Braithwaite won gold in the trap shooting event, his achievement represents one of the last occasions in the history of the Olympic Games in which a gifted amateur with steely determination and great skill won over a field consisting predominantly of commercially sponsored and government funded professionals.

In 1968 Rodney Pattisson and Ian MacDonald-Smith won the gold medal in the Flying Dutchman class in the Olympic Games on their boat called the wonderful 'Supercalifragilisticexpialidocious',

Derek Allhusen riding Lochinvar, Richard Meade riding Cornishman and V, Reuben Jones riding The Poacher won the Eventing Team Gold.

"Spectators seem to forget that boxing is an exercise in self-defence"

THE BRICKLAYER NICKED IT ALL RIGHT . .

CHRIS FINNEGAN, a handsome, blond bricklayer from Iver, Bucks, is the first British boxer to reach the Olympic Games middleweight final since Melbourne in 1956.

From PETER WILSON
Mexico City, Friday

Britain's Chris Finnegan lands a short left to the head of America's Alfred Jones during their middleweight semi-final.

SLICK

EXERCISE

£150-a-week bid for Ben

QUIZ WORD

THE MOST GOLDEN MOMENT OF ALL

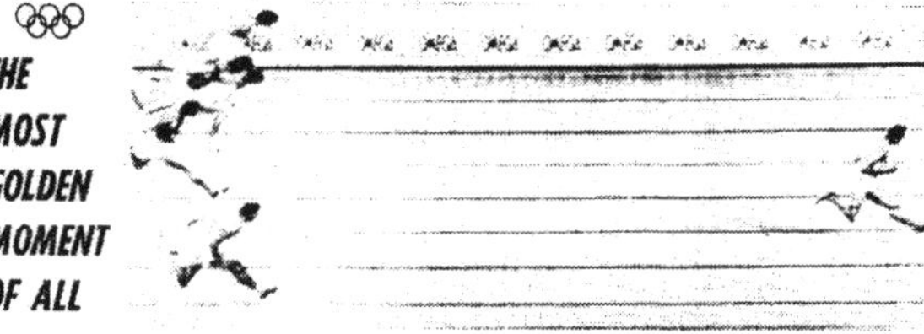

THIS was how Britain's David Hemery pulverised the field in the 400 metres hurdles. . . THIS was how far behind he left them, as he smashed the world record by seven-tenths of a second. And John Sherwood (nearest camera) got up to give Britain the bronze medal as well.

Photo-finish Alan keeps our bold team fighting on . .

BRITAIN'S ATHLETICS team, clearly established as one of the big successes of these Olympics, is treading on air and dreaming of more gold medals.

From PETER WILSON
Mexico City, Wednesday

Improved

Bounced

ALAN PASCOE

RIGHT ON THE NOSE, CARTER!

Mexico City, Wednesday

'SIR DAVID'—IS THE WRITING ON THE WALL

From FRANK McGHEE Mexico City, Wednesday

Lillian sparks off our super show

From PETER WILSON, Mexico City, Monday

BRITAIN'S ATHLETES have exploded into superb shows on this second day of the Olympics. David Hemery and John Sherwood are through to tomorrow's final of the 400 metres hurdles. Della James and Valerie Peat have dashed to the semi-finals of the 100 metres.

LILLIAN BOARD

BIG-HOPE HEMERY POWERS TO FINAL —RECORDS FOR THE SPRINT GIRLS

Campbell left out of draw

Assistance

Surged

Another victim of the altitude . . . Nigeria's Olajumoke Bodunrin crumples at the track-side after her 400 metres bid. And Josero Vincent (Uruguay) is helped away with a pulled muscle.

RESULTS

MEDALS TABLE

AFTER FIRST DAY

WALLER'S FIGHT ENDS IN A BROKEN LEG

From FRANK McGHEE, Mexico City, Monday

TODAY IN MEXICO

EPITAPH

PETER WILSON says: Mexico was not properly geared to staging this extravaganza

Mexico City, Monday.

THE XIXth Olympic Games of the modern era are over. The flame has died, as the sunset dies, but the Olympic trust has been passed on to Munich, in promise of a twentieth dawn in four years' time.

It remains only to write an epitaph for the first Games to be held in the American Continent outside the U.S.A.

National flags are paraded for the last time. Goodbye to Mexico, 1968—and on to Munich.

GAMES THAT MOCKED AT SO MANY HOPES

INCOMPETENT

COMPARISONS

'DARK HORSE'

BIG LET-DOWN

Highlights of the Olympics'

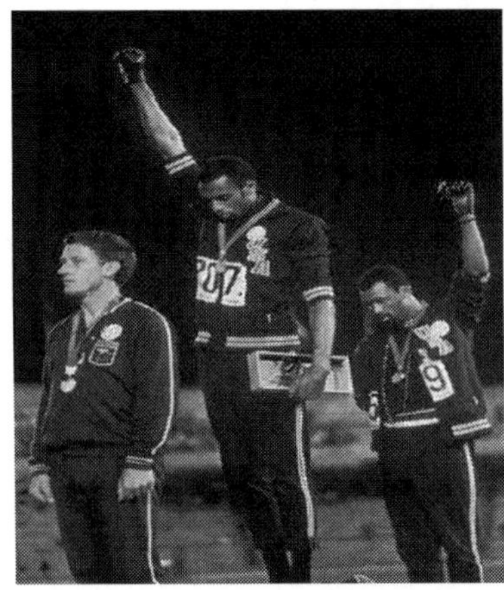

In the medal award ceremony for the men's 200-meter race, black American athletes Tommie Smith (gold) and John Carlos (bronze) took a stand for civil rights by raising their black-gloved fists and wearing black socks in lieu of shoes. The Australian Peter Norman, who had run second, wore an American "civil rights" badge as support to them on the podium. As punishment, the IOC banned Smith and Carlos from the Olympic Games for life, and Norman was left off Australia's Olympic team in 1972.

OLYMPIC COMMENTARY

WILL MANKIND EVER GROW UP?

TO ANYONE who was in Berlin in 1936, the demonstration which Tommie Smith and John Carlos put on in Mexico City in 1968 meant a multitude of different things.

An optimist would have sighed, a pessimist laughed, a philosopher shrugged. It was, according to how you are constituted, ironic, tragic, farcical or inevitable.

By PETER WILSON

IRONIC

COURAGE

CHARADE

COSTLY

Gloved fists raised in a parody of a Nazi salute, Tommie Smith (centre) and John Carlos (right) show their scorn as the American flag is raised. The third man on the rostrum, Peter Norman, the Australian silver medallist, also wore a Black Power badge.

"All this drama took my mind back more than three decades"

Daily Mirror

Saturday, October 19, 1968

Manchester (STD code 061) 832-3444

Black Power athletes told:

GET OUT IN 48 HOURS

From FRANK McGHEE and BRIAN HITCHEN

Mexico City, Friday

YOU have 48 hours to get out of Mexico. That was the order given to America's 200 metre gold medal winner Tommie Smith and bronze medal man John Carlos by the U S Olympics Committee here today.

US Olympic Committee ban Smith and Carlos

Expulsion

Threatened

John Carlos and his wife leave the Olympic Village after Carlos had been ordered out of Mexico by the U.S. Olympic Committee for his part in a Black Power demonstration.

MEXICO '68

—REPORT FROM PETER WILSON

Boulter and Whetton in semi

MEXICO CITY Friday

Dropped

BRILLIANT ALEX HANDS OUT MEDAL WARNING

MEXICO CITY, Friday

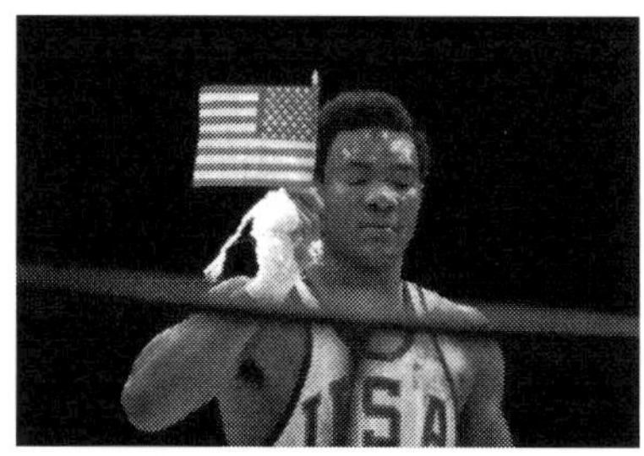

George Foreman won the gold medal for boxing (Heavyweight Division) by defeating Soviet Ionas Chepulis, when the referee stopped the fight in the 2nd round After the victory, Foreman waved a small American flag as he bowed to the crowd.

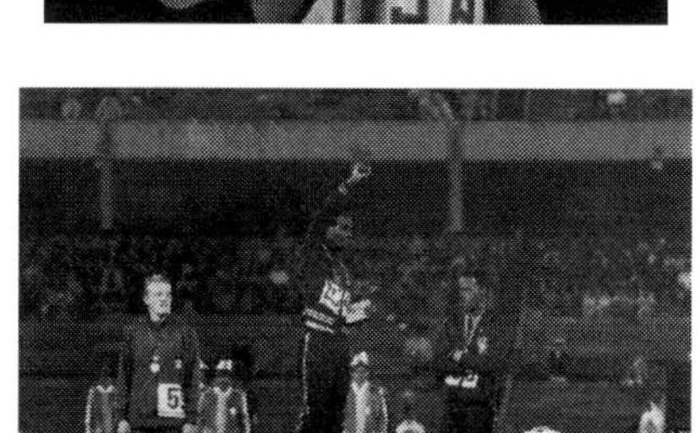

Bob Beamon of the U.S. leapt 8.90 m (29.2 ft) in the long jump, an incredible 55 cm (22 in) improvement over the previous world record. It remained the Olympic record and stood as the world record for 23 years, until broken by American Mike Powell in 1991.

Al Oerter of the U.S. won his fourth consecutive gold medal in the discus to become only the second athlete to achieve this feat in an individual event, and the first in track & field.

Dick Fosbury of the U.S. won the gold medal in the high jump using his unconventional Fosbury flop technique, which quickly became the dominant technique in the event.

The introduction of doping tests resulted in the first person to be disqualified because of doping: Swedish pentathlete, Hans-Gunnar Liljenwall was disqualified for alcohol use (he drank two beers just prior to competing).

I am from Lincoln, UK, born and breed and I have watch and supported Lincoln City through thick and thin for many years and could help myself and having a look back at Lincoln City fifty years ago when they finished 13th in the old fourth division.
I hope you have enjoyed this look at sporting year of 1968 as much as I have.

Lincoln's Badge

Lincoln City 1967/68

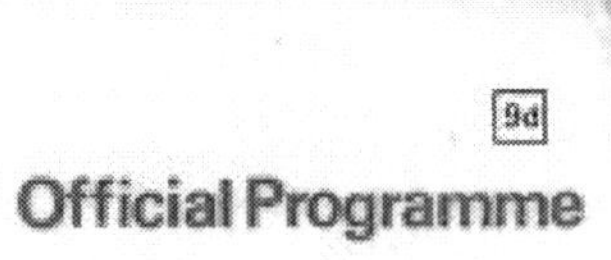
9d

Official Programme

LINCOLN CITY
FOOTBALL CLUB

YORK CITY

Programme

Cartoon

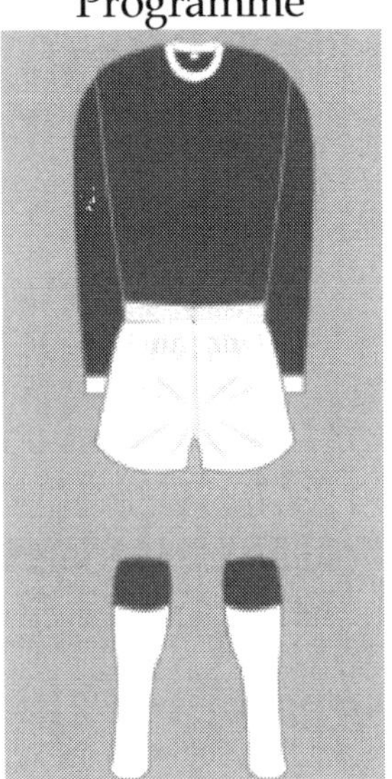

Lincoln's Kit

Jim Grummett, The Lincoln captain

Alf Garnett from tv series Till Does Us Part at West Ham

Printed in Great Britain
by Amazon